Julia Clements Book of Rose Arrangements

Julia Clements Book of Rose Arrangements

B T BATSFORD LTD   LONDON

© Julia Clements 1984
First published 1984
All rights reserved. No part of this publication
may be reproduced, in any form or by any means,
without permission from the Publisher
ISBN 0 7134 4466 5
Printed in Spain
for the publishers by Grijelmo S.A., Bilbao
B T Batsford Ltd
4 Fitzhardinge Street
London W1H 0AH

Frontispiece No studied design was required to create
this picture of roses placed here and there between
stems of Fuchsias in this elegant Edwardian type vase.
  Being woody, split the stem ends of both roses and
Fuschias before placing them in the vase filled with
warm water

Contents

Acknowledgement

My grateful thanks go to:
Thelma M Nye of Batsford for her sympathetic understanding
of my work;
Jon Whitbourne for his excellent colour photography;
Edward Tanner for the black and white photography,
originally taken for *My Roses;*
June Mayhew for wading through my untidy typing and
making it appear clear;
Margaret Stourton for her attractive sketches;
Hamish Haynes for equipment drawings;
and to all rose lovers everywhere who I hope will enjoy this
book.

All the flower arrangements illustrated are by Julia Clements

The badge of England

Introduction

Would you appoint some flower to reign
In matchless beauty on the plain
The Rose (Mankind will all agree)
The Rose, the Queen of Flowers should be

SAPPHO 600 BC

In 1958 I wrote a book on roses or, to be more correct, on rose arrangements. At that time the idea of *arranging* roses, or making a composition of them to suit some title of a show class, was just beginning to permeate the hallowed portals of the Royal National Rose Society. Since then much has happened, much has changed, new varieties of roses have been created, new colours have appeared, shows have assumed a new importance never dreamed of in the days of 'A bowl of roses for effect' when the exhibitor who could show about fifty perfect blooms in a silver bowl won the first prize. No-one stated what *effect* had to be achieved, it was just a bowl of roses which left little room for the new member or the competitor who could only muster about twelve good roses.

Today, with tens of thousands practising the art of arranging roses, schedules have become very sophisticated, with interpretive classes changing each year. Classes are always included to cater for those with small gardens and even for those who do not grow their own roses. However, this book is not only about roses and show work, it is for those who love to have roses in the home, those who love to celebrate with roses, those who love to give roses, those who receive them and, in particular, those who cannot bear to be without them at all times of the year. There are so many ways of using them which, after reading this book, I hope you will try.

The more I travel around my own and other countries,

judging and talking to women's groups, Flower Clubs and Women's Institutes, the more I have become convinced of the tremendous interest there is in the Rose. The questions received from an audience are not only enlightening but often act as a barometer, delineating the trend of thought and interest of the community, and certainly roses have featured high on the list of questions during these last few years; a time which has also witnessed the tremendous growth of interest in the art of flower arranging.

'I wish I could arrange Roses' has been the cry of many new enthusiasts and yet others, with an air of having known and grown roses all their lives, would add 'But do we want to *arrange* roses, aren't they lovely in themselves?'

'Yes, they are,' I have often replied, 'but the more one's horizon is widened, and the more we see of other people's homes and gardens and countries, appreciating their tastes and needs, the more we become conscious of the fact that, fortunately, we do not all want the same thing.' Neither do we all express ourselves in similar fashions. One has only to witness the wealth of ideas shown at the beautiful Flower Arrangement Exhibitions to prove this, and it has always amazed me, when entering one of the Royal National Rose Society's great shows, that so many questions are immediately asked, especially on how best roses can be used in the home.

Perhaps this is easy to understand, for judging by records, there are many more people in the world interested in roses than in any other flower.

Perhaps it is not generally known that in England, the Royal National Rose Society has over 56,000 members. These are enthusiasts who are serious enough to belong to a Society but in addition there are tens of thousands who do not belong. English rose growers send out over half a million catalogues each year and claim to sell millions of rose trees annually. These are sold to rose growers and have no bearing on the millions of cut blooms that are sold each year from the flower markets.

These figures refer only to Britain, but the Rose, with its universal appeal, has as many devotees in other countries. The American Rose Society has 16,000 members, although this does not present a true picture for one grower alone claims to sell 150 million rose trees every year. This I can well believe, for the acreage of some of the American rose nurseries is colossal and it amazed me when visiting them to see tens of thousands of rose trees being kept back in cold storage, waiting shipment to some other part of the United States of America.

The Canadian, New Zealand and Australian Rose Societies all have their thousands of members, as do the Societies in South Africa, France, Japan and Germany. But I do not claim to know where all the 'rosarians' are to be found, I only wish to prove, if proof be necessary, that almost everyone either grows, buys or loves roses. Hence the cry so often heard 'I wish I could arrange roses'. Well you can, for there is no difference in arranging roses than in arranging any other kind of flower, it is simply displaying them so that they look their best to suit you.

Flower arranging is one of the simplest forms of creative art and each year more and more men and women are gaining self expression through its medium. To become accomplished in this subject (which also plays such an important part in interior decorating) is only a question of appreciating a few basic principles of design and colour, added to which is needed a little practice in working technique.

But there is nothing complicated about it, and you need to have no special flair, in fact I have seen some women emerge as great artists with flowers after only a short while; women who, in the beginning appeared to have little idea how to start. The sense of achievement that is felt and shown on the face of a newcomer to this art after she has made her first 'piece' is very rewarding – rewarding to me especially who, in the beginning of my own career, felt a similar sense of fulfilment every time I faced and won over a new audience with my simple approach to this subject. So simple that thousands since have been convinced that they too can do it. And so they can.

Perhaps the best advice I can offer those who are not already practised is 'Enjoy your flower arranging'. Learn the basic principles, yes, for they will prove to be a good standby when in doubt, but as soon as you are well practised in them, shed them and allow yourself to *feel*, enjoy what you feel.

As a judge, I can always discern when a competitor has enjoyed making her design as against another who has tried hard to follow the rules, but this state of relaxed enjoyment can only be reached after a study of the groundwork has been covered.

This book, as you will now have gathered, is not about the growing of roses – there are so many excellent publications on the market today dealing with their cultivation – but it *does* set out to widen your interest in roses.

Not only in its pages have I tried to give you ideas for their use in the home, and at shows, but also I have included chapters on the very items which really gave birth to this book, as well as a number of fascinating discoveries – discoveries that I have long wanted to share with my many flower loving friends all over the world.

In compiling this book I have also been given a chance to answer my many followers and friends who write and ask if there is any particular foliage that should not be put with roses, and if there is any special type of vase that should be used for roses. And always there is the cry 'Can they be made to last longer?'

All of these questions and many more will be answered in the following pages and I sincerely trust, as you glance through the sections, that you will become more and more convinced that whether you pick, buy or grow your roses, arranging them is not only a creative art, but also a most satisfying expression which can be practised by all.

Chelsea, London 1984   *Julia Clements*

Arranging Roses

The Rose doth deserve the chief and prime place among all Floures whatsoever: being not only esteemed for his beauty vertues and his fragrant and odiferous smell: but also because it is the honour and ornament of our English scepter…which pleasant floures deserve the chiefest place in crownes and garlands.

JOHN GERARD

You can arrange roses in any way you like. There are no set rules. Many people will place a bunch of roses into a container and all will agree how lovely they look. In such cases they are looking at the roses. But if you are interested in the *art* of arranging flowers, which is a self-expressive subject, you will want to put a little of *yourself* into the design of the arrangement, so that the final result is one which is expressive of you. You may like a certain colour which means *you,* you may prefer a certain style, you may like to include fruit with your roses for a table decoration; but no matter what you do, if you are *thinking* and putting your heart into it whilst you are working you will create a picture all your own.

At this stage, let me state there are three main styles of arranging roses (1) the formal style (2) the modern style (3) table arrangements. All can be adapted to big or small, round or oblong, high or low. After that, when you have acquired the technique of getting the roses into the container you are on your own, and you can create any style you like. Call it free style, or one of your own, and it will be quite right for you.

Formal style

However, in teaching, let us look at the formal style. Having prepared your roses as stated on page 00, and having chosen your colour and the setting in which the finished design will stand, prepare your container. Either pour in sufficient tepid water to prevent the stems drying out and fill in with crumpled wire netting (2 in.- 5 cm mesh) or use a block of water-soaked floral foam held down to the vase with florist's tape or clear adhesive tape. In both cases it should reach about an inch – 25mm above the rim. You then start to make the framework or outline of your arrangement with the tallest plant material; this could be buds, or sprays of fine foliage. You can make the height to suit your setting; it can be tall for a high-ceilinged room or a pedestal, or shorter for a side table.

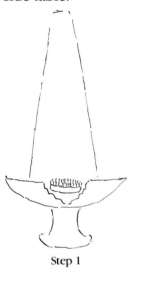

Step 1

Step 2

Step 3

Step 1   Cut a block of wet *Oasis* in the shape of a cone and press it on to a large pinholder standing in the base of a container

Step 2   Insert roses all round here and there, placing peaches (not compulsory) round the base

Step 3   For final effect, and to break up the even outline, add stems of honeysuckle or any other fine greenery

13

A gilded urn holds this design of pale yellow *Vanda Beauty* roses, the outline being made with Stephanandra foliage. These roses were cut to different levels, the lower ones flowing forward. The urn was filled with crumpled wire netting which holds the stems firmly in place

A block of *Oasis* can be held firm in the vase by placing a strip of clear adhesive tape over the foam, pressing the tape to each side of the vase. Do this crosswise and not straight over the top, for you will need the centre to insert the main flowers

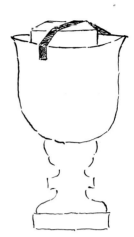

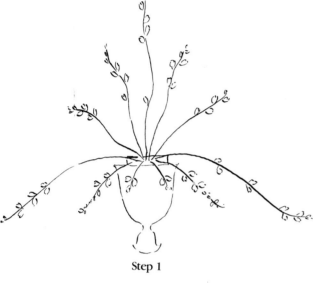

Step 1

Step 2

 Step 1   The outline of any large design is made by creating height and width with fine foliage or branches, all the stems emerging from a focal point at the base of the tall central stem

Step 2   Insert the larger, or more open roses, in the centre, the lower ones protruding forward. Finally (not shown) fill in from the outside to the centre

15

Having made the outline, try to place your biggest or more important roses down the centre, tilting some of the stems forward and cutting some stems shorter than the others so that no two heads stand level with the other. You can now place extra leaves around the low centre to emphasise it (the centre of interest or focal point is always underneath the tallest point). You can then fill in with the rest of the roses, working from the outside to the centre, at the same time making sure that some of the lowest flowers flow forward over the rim of the container. To avoid a flat back, add more leaves or shorter roses. In the final appearance the roses should be so inserted in the container that they appear to flow out from the central point or converge on it. It is for this reason that the centre is emphasised in some way whether with larger flowers or extra leaves or fruit, for this emphasis unites all the stems. Sometimes the roses are used mainly for the centre of an arrangement when taller flowers, such as Delphiniums, Larkspur, or Monbretia, are used to form the outline.

Mixed buxom hybrid tea roses fill this white china vase, the foliage being placed first. Wire netting holds the stems in place. Notice how each head is fully visable by cutting each stem shorter than the other

Modern style

This follows a similar pattern in as much as there is (1) height, (2) fill in and (3) main interest. You can establish the height (again to suit your setting) with bullrushes, branches, twigs or wood. Roses can be placed in between and lower, and leaves can be inserted low down, or, in place of leaves, stones, shells or chunks of wood can be used.

A simple modern design can be achieved by inserting a swerving branch on to a pinholder set in the base of a container

Step 2 Add an interesting leaf such as Fatzia or Bergenia and three roses set at different levels

Here the lovely hybrid tea rose *Pascali* is combined with a dry honeysuckle branch and fresh flowering honeysuckle strands. The tall tubular container was two thirds filled with sand on which a dish holding *Oasis* was stood. The dry twisted branch was placed across the mouth of the container it needing no more support, and the roses and honeysuckle flowers were inserted in between

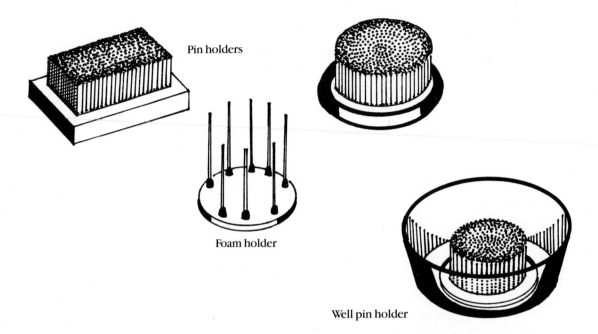

Pin holders

Foam holder

Well pin holder

A pinholder is mainly used to hold the stems in place (a 3½ in. – 9cm size is better than a smaller one) and if the material is inserted in the order of (1) tall (2) medium and (3) short, covering the holder low down with either leaves, wood or stones you cannot go wrong. However, remember that modern design requires fewer roses, there should be some linear pattern and please do leave space here and there, in other words, do not fill in all the 'holes'. Containers of modern pottery are helpful to emphasise the style and small dishes on wooden bases are often used. So many people are good at improvising and you have only to visit any flower arrangement or rose show to see how many variations of modern containers can be made, even from household utensiles.

Tendrils of Salix were sprayed with silver paint and used to give height and background to the pink roses placed in a dish of water behind the cluster of shells which stand on a perspex disc over a rose-coloured base. More short roses and leaves flow out at the back

Table arrangements

The principles of outline, fill in and focal interest can again be employed when making a table arrangement. You can make an elongated triangle (if you want to see over it) or you can make a round effect by shortening the sides, or create an oblong by lengthening the sides, but the individual touches of what you put into it yourself will make the success of your design. You may choose an unusual colour, or a new rose (this will create a talking point especially if you know its name and where it can be obtained). You may add, for example, some pale green grapes to cream coloured roses. A contrasting coloured base may appeal to you or a tall candle rising from a circlet of roses might be your choice. The ideas for table designs are endless and can be varied as often as the menu. The mention of menus reminds me that a dinner party can also be made memorable if a contrasting coloured cloth is used with your roses. Try an apple green cloth with white roses for a summer luncheon party or pale pink roses on a deeper pink cloth. Red roses on a gold lamé cloth is an idea for a golden wedding party, and wide ribbons stretching down the length of a satin cloth, on which roses are placed, makes an unusual touch for a birthday party. Matching or contrasting candles are an ideal combination with roses and cut-out roses appliquéd onto a muslin cloth will give a touch of elegance. Matching your roses with some touch of colour in the table china will put a personal touch to your scheme, especially if the roses can be arranged in the vegetable tureen standing on the meat dish.

 In a shallow silver dish, these short stems from a head of the floribunda rose *Fleur Cowles* make an ideal effect for a dining table when candles are placed each side

Step 1   Place a dowel stick into a wodge of plasticine in the base of a pot, then surround it with stones and fill the pot with plaster filler powder, or cement powder, mixed with water to a stiff consistency. Place a block of wet *Oasis* on the top of the stick and cover it with wire netting. this will avoid it slipping down

Step 2   Insert short roses into the *Oasis* and finish at the base with a bow of ribbon. This is ideal for small party tables, or for a number to be placed down a long table

Step 1   For a lower centre table arrangement, insert the first five stems as shown in the drawing

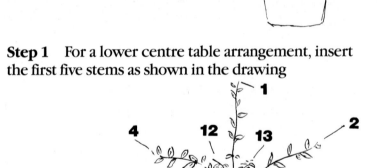

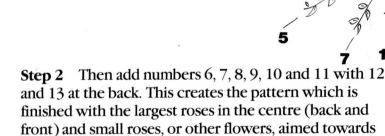

Step 2   Then add numbers 6, 7, 8, 9, 10 and 11 with 12 and 13 at the back. This creates the pattern which is finished with the largest roses in the centre (back and front) and small roses, or other flowers, aimed towards the centre

24

 Close-up of table centrepiece using old fashioned roses, now so popular, with grapes held firm in wet *Oasis* in a silver dish *See also page 46.*

I keep a number of different coloured lengths of twill, satin or silk jersey to use as cloths. I have even cold dyed a sheet on occasions to obtain the exact shade I needed. Another idea, if you are a keen rose grower, is to place or scatter rose petals on the cloth first, covering it with muslin or fine net. If using candelabras on a table, again place the finest plant material on the outside, using the larger flowers or roses near the centre. Candle cups (from the florist or garden centre or flower club) are used to hold the candles and flowers in a candelabra arrangement. The candle cup is pressed into the candlestick and held firm by plasticine or tied down with fuse wire. Fill the candle cup with floral foam or wire netting and proceed as for a low table arrangement. Whatever you do, try not to leave your table flowers to the last moment. Prepare them the night before, giving them a long deep drink and make your table design in the morning according to the size and shape of the table, remembering other items will later be placed on it.

Pot et fleur style

Few flowers lend themselves as well as roses to the *pot et fleur* style of home decoration. Such a style is a semi-permanent grouping of pot plants with cut roses added. The plants, which should be put together in one container, should have variety and contrast of texture, ie perhaps one tall one, another broad leaved, and other trailing and perhaps another as a filler. They can be in pots, or planted in soil in the overall container, and space should be left for either a tube to be inserted to hold cut roses in water, or a piece of *Oasis* held in a tin of water and set among the plants to do the same. A branch or piece of driftwood may be added, but **no** cut foliage. The plants can be left *in situ* and the roses changed as desired.

 A bunch of ten *Sonia* roses from the florist is here combined with a maidenhair plant, asparagus and fruit to form this Pot et Fleur arrangement. Wet *Oasis* fills the bowl on which the plant stands, the roses, and applies on sticks, being inserted separately

 The delicate sweet smelling *Margaret Merrill* rose is here used in a brown dish with white Hebe for this cream and brown table setting with matching candles and candle sticks

 Pink *Garnette* roses are used in this table design for a wedding. The roses were inserted into a block of *Oasis* balanced on the right with a full bow of apple-green ribbon which matches the candle

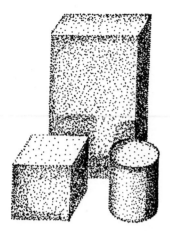

Blocks of foam marketed under several trade names such as *Oasis, Flora foam, Bloomlife* and *Sylvia*

Roses with other flowers and foliage

Some of the most attractive flower decorations are composed of summer and even autumn flowers combined with roses as the main interest.

As early as late spring or early summer a few branches of Philadelphus (mock orange-syringa) can be picked to form the framework of large or small groups. A background spread of these creamy white blossoms used in a church for a wedding pedestal group combined with cream or pink roses makes a romantic sight. Similar groups used for the reception, placed on the mantleshelf or on a pedestal, always evokes admiration, and if this becomes your choice for some event, do remove some of the green leaves of the Philadelphus in order to play up the pink and white effect. Try to pick the Philadelphus in bud, then after removing some of the leaves, split the stem ends and stand them in deep warm water to which some sugar is added (dessert spoonful to a bucketful) and leave them for some hours; in this way, the water channel will become filled, so helping the blossom to last longer. The same treatment should be given to the roses, then, when ready, make whatever shape you desire with the branches, tilting some forward, some backward, adding the roses centrally and in between the blossom. Similar light effects can be obtained with branches and twigs of lime: stripped of their green leaves, the pale yellow/green flower is left which creates a magical effect. I have used lime flowers with the creamy/pink *Fleur Cowles* rose to great effect and never tire of this combination. Writing of lime green reminds me of that every-popular flower Alchemilla mollis (Lady's mantle). A bowl of this frothy green flower interspersed with roses is sheer delight. I am reminded also of another low-table arrangement I saw in a friend's house made with a mass of

An unusual centre piece can be made by standing a cone of wet *Oasis* on a heavy pinholder which in turn is stood on a white china cake stand. The roses, *Fleur Cowle,* are inserted at intervals all round with greenery close in to cover the *Oasis,* and stems of honeysuckle break up the evenness of the outline. A few peaches were added low down in the design

Gypsophila and red polyantha roses. Red and white has never been my choice of colour combination, remembering the superstition of hospital nurses, yet this looked really lovely and so delicate.

Referring to the flowering branches already mentioned I must also mention the lovely swerving sprays of Deutzia in its various colours and the spicy smelling sprays of Ribes (flowering currant). Some I know, do not like the smell of this flowering shrub, but I love it. I cannot leave reference to these flowering shrubs without mention of the dainty Spirea (bridal wreath). This shrub with its graceful arching stems makes a perfect foil for pink roses. We must not forget that many of these attractive flowering shrubs bloom early – about April, May or June, therefore are very suitable for roses bought from the florist.

In contrast one has only to look round the gardens in summer to see how many of the border flowers will combine so well with roses. Flowers, such as Delphiniums, Larkspur, Astilbes, Arunculas are all suitable and if your garden does not produce the flowers you might need, there are often many attractive leaves available. Golden Privet, makes an ideal background for yellow or flame-coloured roses, and the addition of some broad leaves such as Hosta or Fatzia will give depth to a design of all round roses.

The art of flower arranging is composed of using different forms, shapes and sizes, so some tall leaves will give *points,* against the *rounds* of the roses, and some flat leaves will give *depth* to your design.

This formal triangular style is composed of *Queen Elizabeth* roses backed by Stephanandra foliage and interspersed with Alchemilla mollis (Lady's mantle). The triangular outline is made with the foliage and the roses cut to different levels, the lower one tilting forward. Remember to place shorter roses, and foliage flowing backwards, to avoid a flat back

Roses with candles

There is probably no more delightful decoration in the home than a combination of roses with candles. Candles today are made in every conceivable shape, size and colour so one need never be at a loss to decide what to put with a few roses. In colour, candles can add contrast or harmony. Some of the new Prices' pastel coloured candles are sheer delight. Candles can give height to a low grouping of roses. Try putting three pink candles into a block of water-soaked *Oasis* standing in a low dish, then insert short stems of deeper pink and crimson floribunda roses to cover the *Oasis* from all sides. Brown candles are also ideal to combine with yellow and flame-coloured roses, in fact on one occasion I used a grouping of cream, brown and flame candles with that lovely *Grandpa Dickson* rose, although some of my friends said they would have preferred to see all brown candles. As with everything, it is a matter of personal choice.

Another idea, when only a few roses are available, is to press a small block of wet *Oasis* on to a pinholder, standing this on a cake stand. Next place a chunky candle on the top of the *Oasis,* and finish by covering the foam with short-stemmed roses. As many of these chunky candles last a great number of hours, (some of them up to 72 hours), they make an ideal centrepiece or small hall decoration.

I am very fond of lime-green candles, feeling that this colour associates with almost any colour rose, but if a harmonious colour scheme is your choice for a table decoration it is well worth visiting one of the stores, for the colour range today is enormous. The glow which lighted candles produce adds a touch of intimacy which other forms of lighting seem to disperse and for this reason, in autumn and winter when the bulk of summer roses are over, a few blooms with colourful candles will, I am sure, delight everyone.

If the pressing of flowers is one of your hobbies, rose petals can be used to decorate the sides of the candle. The almost dry rose petals can be glued to the sides of the candle, and once firmly in place they can be covered with varnish or melted candle wax. Melt some odd ends of ordinary white candles then, with a brush, cover the petals, this has to be

 Thalictrum flavum was inserted for height in this casual arrangement of *Sunblest* roses held in a block of water-soaked *Oasis* in a copper pot. The round heads if Bupleurum fruticosum (they turn yellow in Autumn) were interspersed, and sprigs of honeysuckle completed the effect. Crumpled wire netting can be used equally well to hold the stems in place

done *very quickly,* otherwise the wax will set, try to use quick, firm brush strokes from top to bottom covering the petals.

If the candles are too large for the candlestick, dip the ends in very hot water for a few minutes, then press them firmly in place and in the absence of a candle holder, when using *Oasis* bind four cocktail sticks or hairpins round the end of the candle with adhesive tape or wire, the protruding prongs can then be inserted into the *Oasis* to hold the candle upright.

To help your candles last longer, keep them in the fridge for some hours before lighting them and, if you want to avoid spilling wax when extinguishing the candles, try blowing across your forefinger held horizontally across your mouth.

This party buffet arrangement is made in a candle cup inserted into the centre opening of a three-branch candelabrum. The centre cup was filled with *Oasis* the ivy and pinks flowing downwards Roses form the main central interest whilst fruit is grouped around the base

 Pink *Garnette* roses are here held in a small dish filled with *Oasis* on a pinholder and placed at the side of a white tray. The space gives importance to the few roses

 Pink and crimson old shrub roses are here held in a shallow dish containing *Oasis* over a pinholder. Combined with green glasses, and stood at the left of the base, the effect is finished by the addition of a green candle

Roses with wood

Many rustic settings and some modern ones also are most suitable for designs of roses with wood. In fact a piece of wood, if sand blasted or smoothed and polished and set on a base and finally adorned with one or two roses, would be equally at home in a formal setting. So open your eyes to the possibilities of using 'found wood' as part of your design with roses. A piece of 'found wood', 'driftwood' or 'Nature's Sculpture in wood', call it what you will, if set on a base, garnished with a few roses set in a well pinholder, will quickly become a talking point among family and friends.

'Driftwood' is the term mainly used for wood washed up by the sea shore or found on the banks of lakes and lochs. This has often been weathered by sea and sun, which produces a greyish patina, whereas the wood which is found in woodlands by broken boughs, upturned trees, roots, etc, should be treated. Interesting shapes can also be found among the roots of tree ivy. In this case, the roots should be soaked in strong soda water overnight, and the bark peeled off the next morning. This will leave the shiny cream interior which can be bleached, or painted to suit your wishes. Pieces of wood picked up in the countryside or woods should first be soaked in disinfectant to kill any lurking bugs, then all the soft wood should be scraped away with a knife, and finally left to dry. It can be treated finally with linseed oil to avoid unnecessary cracks, or it can be varnished or painted, but any piece of wood should be valued, for it is sure to find its way into a decoration with roses at some time. Dry roots, or vines can give height, width or contrast of texture when combined with roses. Every piece of found wood is different. It can be placed upright or lengthwise, and should difficulty be found in making the wood stand firm, try sawing off pieces to give a firm base, or bore a hole in the main piece

 Four *Sonia* roses from the florist are here placed in a well holder (or a pinholder in a shallow tin) set behind some interesting tree stump placed on a brown velvet base. The tall bleached branches were inserted first and leaves were finally placed at the back and sides to cover the holder

and insert a dowl stick, or screw a flat stand to the main wood, to help it stand upright and firm. It all depends upon the shape of your piece of wood. Most of the fun is in trying different ways of using it. You might simply varnish it, or might rub it over with coloured shoe polish to accent a colour scheme, you could lightly spray paint it with two different colours. Pastel chalks rubbed into the cracks of 'found wood' also gives interesting results. Another good idea to give colour but which does not conceal the texture of the wood, is to make up a mixture of one cup of clear ammonia, two tablespoonsful of copper powder (from hardware or art shops) and two or three tablespoonsful of white glue. The wood should be painted with this and as it dries the mixture will oxidise, and assume an eerie blue/green patina. I used half of this quantity to cover a tall piece of driftwood, and the result was delightful, so the amount you make will depend upon the size of the surface you have to cover.

In addition to wood, roses can be associated with glass, china, pottery, pebbles, ornaments, shells and all kinds of other objects. It all depends upon your mood as what roses you combine with what.

 This piece of ivy root pulled from a tree and stripped of its bark, was finally painted black and fixed to a base of wood with a strong glue such as *Araldite*. A small block of wet *Oasis* wrapped in plastic was inserted between the crevices, and flowing stems of honeysuckle form a background to the few red roses in this modern design

The Old Fashioned Shrub Roses

Roses, the garden's pride
Are flowers for love and flowers for kings.
Now hath Flora

THOMAS CAMPION 1567-1620

Old fashioned roses' is a loose term used by many when referring to the old shrub roses. Many of these shrub roses bloom only once a year but their blooms are so exquisite that they are again becoming popular. Many make marvellous garden plants but here I want to refer to some of these gems for decoration in the home. They are without doubt the connoisseur's rose, in fact the term 'one upmanship' is often applied to those who grow, know and understand the old shrub roses. The history of the rose is fascinating, dating back to long before Christ. In fact rose fossil remains have been discovered by geologists as early as the Tertiary period, but most of the old shrub roses now available were bred in the nineteenth century.

I was reminded of this some years ago when I remarked to a grower that I would like to grow some of the old Bourbon roses. He was interested and asked if I might like to have some of the earlier ones. He then went on to explain that prior to the Bourbons in the history of the rose there were the *Chinas*, the *Damasks*, the *Musks* and the *Gallicas*, the latter being probably the oldest in Europe. I then wondered about the Moss rose and he explained that this came down from the Centifolias, which descended from the Albas and which in turn came from the Dog rose and the Damask. He noticed my perplexity also my interest and suggested that if I

Here a mixed group of old fashioned shrub roses are held in by wire netting in a glass bowl of water standing on a silver tray, suitable for a dining table centre piece. The roses include the pink *Fantin Latour, Tuscany Superb,* and the creamy-yellow *Fruhlingsgold.* A low bowl can be flanked by tall candelabra to give three dimensions to the table setting

wanted to know more about these fascinating roses I should read Michael Gibson's book *Shrub Roses for Every Garden**. I since have and with relish.

I wondered afterwards why so many of these old roses have French names. It appears that as so many of them were raised in France at the time of the Empress Josephine and throughout the nineteenth century it was obvious they would carry French names. It was the Empress who formed a unique collection of all the rose species and varieties that were then available at her home at Malmaison outside Paris, and so made the roses a fashionable garden flower.

Most of these roses can be seen growing in the gardens of the Royal National Rose Society at Chiswell Green Lane, St Albans in Hertfordshire, and few visitors to London fail to visit the magnificent Queen Mary's rose gardens in Regents Park where roses bloom in abundance.

For my part I love to see these 'old fashioneds' in the home and to gaze upon them. Just one, two or perhaps three. They are so exquisite, such miracles of nature, that a warming sense of wonderment comes from contemplating these beauties that have survived these thousands of years. I am among many who claim *Rose Mundi*, a Gallica, as a favourite. I love its striped pink or crimson and white petals. *Reine de Violettes* is another popular old rose because of its deep purplish colouring. *Boule de Neige* is an exquisite white and *Variegata di Bologna*, a Bourbon, is loved by many decorators for its crimson/purplish stripes on a lilac/white background. A few of any of these old roses placed on a low table is sure to attract attention, which will in turn lead the onlookers to discover more about these exquisite roses, nearly all of which are highly scented.

 By using a pinholder in a shallow dish of water or water-soaked *Oasis,* a few roses – I used *Julia's Rose* – can be inserted, and surrounded with fruit for a low table design

46

 Margaret Merrill is the name of the creamy-white rose used in this asymmetrical design. Held in wet *Oasis,* the roses are backed with variegated privet with ivy dropping down at the right

Care of cut roses for arrangements

Many people leave their roses in the garden until they are almost fully open, then decide to cut and bring them indoors. It is no wonder that they do not last long in the house because they were almost at the end of their life when they were cut. So, cutting roses for indoor arrangement is a question of timing.

When cutting roses from the bush, cut just above a leaf joint leaving space for new shoots

When and how to cut roses

To enjoy roses in the house as well as the garden, try to cut them late in the evening or early morning when transpiration is at its lowest. Do not wait for them to be fully open but pick or cut some in bud and some half open; like this you will have a variation of form when they are arranged.

Cut just above a leaf joint when cutting from the garden; this will allow another shoot to grow. Try to study the shape and size of the bush when cutting, ie cut one or two roses if the bush is new or small, although you could cut a third of the bush if it is large and well established. Most roses last well in water but do not pick them for show purposes when they are past their prime. If the tips of the stamens of open roses are brown or dry, it usually means the bees have pollinated them, which in turn means they will begin to fade as their role in life has been fulfilled. Hybrid tea roses and the Garnette type of rose last very well when cut. It was noticed that the milk chocolate parchment-brown *Julia's Rose* lasted another week when taken home after five days on show at the Royal Horticultural Society's Chelsea Flower Show. Although wide open, the petals did not drop.

Floribunda roses are excellent for arranging but the cluster heads do need to be thinned out. Try to cut out the more fully opened blooms, leaving room for the buds to open or expand as they grow. The blooms that are removed need not be wasted, for they can be used in small table decorations or floated in a shallow dish of water, held up by their own leaves.

When you are faced with a heavy cluster of roses, such as with many floribundas, trim off some of the short roses leaving a longer finer stem which can be used on the outside of the arrangement. The roses removed can either be tucked into the design, or used in another smaller arrangement

Scrape off the thorns with a sharp knife to allow easier insertion into the wire netting or floral foam

Split the stem ends of cut roses to allow for greater intake of water, then leave in deep water for some hours before arranging

 Ideal for an outdoor patio setting, these *Iceberg* roses were inserted into wet *Oasis* in the saucer-like base of the lamp stand

Conditioning cut roses

After cutting, remove lower leaves and scrape off the thorns with the sharp blade of a knife. This will make positioning the roses in the decoration easier. Next split the stem ends with a knife or flower scissors and remove some of the lower leaves and stand them in deep, tepid water for some hours, or overnight if possible, adding some sugar (a teaspoonful to each pint – half litre of water). This long drink will fully charge the stems with water and so help them to remain turgid and strong in the vase. There are several quite effective products on the market for lengthening the life of flowers. If cut roses start to droop at the head, recut the stem ends and stand in very hot water, making sure the steam does not reach the flower head. This removes any air locks and some say it swells the wood, so allowing for a quicker intake of water.

 A few short items of pink *Dearest* roses, were here inserted into wet *Oasis* in this attractive conch shell; first covered inside with two coats of varnish to make it watertight

Roses from the florist

The most popular flower that is sold in the florist shops is, undoubtedly, the Rose. Everyone knows a rose, everyone loves a rose, so it is not surprising that this flower is chosen as a gift for birthdays, weddings, celebrations or a gift to oneself.

Most town people buy roses for any occasion and they make ideal gifts for a dinner party. Millions of roses are sold every year, in fact the British Flower Industry states that roses are the cornerstone of the industry.

They are long lasting, if treated correctly, and whilst the rose from the florist, via the market, via the grower, is slightly different from the garden rose, in as much as it has been grown under glass and will have long straight stems, it will usually have lush clean foliage free from disease.

Why they grow the stems so long I have never understood, for most of us shorten them, but whether you buy a few single roses or a bunch of ten, do in every case recut the stem ends and remove most of the lower foliage. Finally, as for garden roses split the stem ends and stand them in deep tepid water for some hours before arranging them – this will recharge the water channels and help them to last longer. Sometimes the heads droop over – this means they have been picked too soon and although this does not happen often for growers are well aware of all problems – should you receive some in this condition, try cutting off some of the stem ends and stand in almost boiling water for a few minutes. I have a friend who told me she has often had roses delivered to her which have been left outside the door of her flat during her absence at week-ends. On her return they have all drooped and look almost dead. They are not dead, as I have explained, they are only resting, so cut off some of the stem, remove lower leaves and stand them in very hot water to which a teaspoonful of sugar is added – they will soon perk up.

Some of the best sellers all over the country's markets are *Iona*, which is a superb rich red, *Sonio*, a lovely rose which I use often, this is a peachy pink, whilst *Bridal Pink* is a really beautiful pale pink, lovely for a table decoration. *Champagne* is superb for parties and provides a good talking point. Most decorators would choose *Carte Blanche*, a lovely white rose for weddings and for long lasting most would choose the *Garnette* and *Carol* type although these are not long stemmed and are often termed 'miniatures' in the cut flower market, not to be confused by the real 12 in. – 30cm miniatures mentioned in the following section.

Miniature roses

Although I personally cannot vouch for the truth of it, I have been told that miniature roses were much in favour in Victorian times. As with fashions they fell from favour but following a revival in their interest at the end of the First World War they are now enjoying a renewed burst of popularity for indoor decoration. I am referring to the real miniatures, the bushes which grow to about six inches – 15cm and not to the Polyantha varieties or the 'Fairy' type, nor even to the Garnette and Coral varieties.

There are many who, perhaps deprived of a larger garden, love to continue their interest on a smaller scale. However, these small delightful plants should not be treated as house plants for they are hardy, and whilst they will delight you placed in strategic spots in the home, they do enjoy a good spell out of doors, whether it's on a window sill, patio or better still, planted in the garden. (As the flowers fade they should be removed, just as you would cut a fully blown rose on a normal size bush to allow others to open.) Treat and nurture them as you would your familiar garden roses even to the point of picking some blooms for decoration should you wish to do so. If planted in a tub on the patio or in the garden, try to give them a sunny spot, for the more sun the more they flower. Pick some of the roses in various stages of growth, just as you would pick them from the garden, then place the stems in deep tepid water whilst preparing your container. Many items, can be used as containers: receptacles such as snuff boxes, pill boxes, salt cellars, wine glasses, shells, even thimbles, can be brought into play and if the containers are filled with crumpled fuse wire or small pieces of *Oasis*, the tiny flowers will last a long time, especially if they've had a long drink first. Pruning is simply a matter of

Small pieces of *Oasis* were inserted into these charming Royal Worcester salt cellars to hold different groups of miniature roses. Placed here, one above the other for the sake of photography, they could be used each side of a candlestick for a table setting. Soak *Oasis* up to half an hour before using and tie it down with a narrow strip of clear adhesive tape

trimming the plants into shape each winter, until they become too big for their location. Then cut them down quite hard and start all over again. Extra tall shoots may be cut back at any time during the growing season. No need to wait until winter.

These enchanting miniature roses, whether used as a plant in a ramekin as a cache pot or as cut flowers in any small container, will delight all who seem them and when you realise that one rose grower alone, Gregory's of Nottingham who catalogue 24 varieties, sells about 70,000 a year, there must be many happy miniature rose tree owners in the country, and I am one of them. One of my favourites is *Lavender Lace* which is a pale mauve, and I recently stood plants of *Strawberry Whirl* (vanilla pink) placed in coffee cups and saucers each side of a candelabra for a table centrepiece. The candelabra and the cups and saucers were stood on a strawberry coloured velvet base. Other colours which attract me are *Cinderella* (white with touches of pink), *Mood Music*, a peachy/orange and the new *Green Diamond* (pale lime green), but there are so many from which to choose, and they will all delight you.

Most reputable rose growers can supply miniature rose trees in various colours which include the *Sunblaze* range ie *Orange Sunblaze*, *Pink Sunblaze*, *Yellow Sunblaze*, *Royal Baby* and others in the Meilland group.

Containers

The choice of containers for rose arrangements much depends on the setting and the style of home in which the roses are to be seen. There was a time not so many years ago when it was said that roses should only be arranged in silver or glass vases. That view, of course, is far too rigid. Silver, glass, porcelain dishes and fine china are ideal for a formal setting but wood, chunky pottery, steel and rough china containers are more appropriate for a modern atmosphere. In all cases it is better not to use a container which has a highly patterned surface for this will conflict with the roses.

 The beautiful yellow *Peer Gynt* rose is here inserted on to a pinholder placed in the top of the Clive Brooker pottery container. Cane from a craft shop is twisted in and around to soften the effect, the ends finally being inserted in the pinholder

Colours

The colour of the roses you use depends upon personal choice or the occasion for which they are intended. Many people do not accept the trend towards blue roses and others abhor the browny, grey, parchment and lilac colourings, referring to them as insipid. It all depends on whether you need a strong colour impact in the garden or a display of subtle colour in home decoration. However, for decorators a great deal will depend upon the lasting quality of the roses. A list of suitable roses is given below. In addition to these there are several attractive bi-coloured shrub and climber roses.

Garden roses for cutting

Floribundas

PINK
Pink Parfait
Queen Elizabeth
Dearest
Paddy McGredy (pinky red)
Fleur Cowles (cream-pink)

DEEP AND LIGHT RED
Rob Roy
Lilli Marlene
Evelyn Fison
Rosemary Rose
Marlena
City of Belfast

YELLOW
Arthur Bell
Allgold
Golden Delight
Golden Treasure

SALMON/CORAL/ORANGE/FLAME
Pineapple Poll
Woburn Abbey
Joseph's Coat
Elizabeth of Glamis
Ann Aberconway

CREAM AND WHITE
Iceberg
Moon Maiden
White Spray
Penelope
Margaret Merrill

UNUSUAL COLOURS
News (purple-red)
Lilac Charm (lilac-mauve)
Ripples (wavy petalled, mauve)
Silver Charm (lilac)
Grey Dawn (soft grey)
Jocelyn (mahogany)
Amberlight (golden brown)
Julia's Rose
   (chocolate/parchment)
Brown Velvet (brown)

Hybrid Teas

YELLOW AND CREAM
Grandpa Dickson
Peace
Sutter's Gold
Young Quinn
Diorama
Sunsilk
Pascali (white)

ORANGE OR TANGERINE/FLAME
Whisky Mac
Doris Tysterman
Bettina
Just Joey
Sir Lancelot
Cheshire Life (orange/vermilion)
Korp

PINK
Blessings
Ballet
Prima Ballerina
Lady Seton (deep pink)
Criterio
Mischief (salmon)
Helen Traubel (coral)

RED
National Trust
Alec's Red
Stanley Gibbons
Fragrant Cloud
Mme Louis Laperriere
Super Star (orange-red)

Here a mixture of floribunda roses are inserted through crumpled wire netting in a vegetable tureen to form a table centrepiece. The netting can be tied down to the tureen to keep it firm whilst inserting the roses. Matching rose plates complete the setting

Show Work

According to Argenaeus, Cleopatra had a floor completely coverd with rose petals in a depth of one and a half feet on which to lie.

Not everyone wishes to exhibit or compete in a show, yet many do. Just as a keen follower of any sport or interest competes to see how he or she fares against another, so also do thousands of rose arrangers enter into competition to test their skill and knowledge. Competition work is different from that which you might do at home (where you can do as you like), for in competition you must follow the dictates of the schedule and in competing you are encouraged to try just that bit harder. It is not always winning a prize that is the real object of entering into competition but the spur of fame attached to it certainly stretches one to do better than before. There is also the cameraderie to be enjoyed at a show, and so much to learn. I have known keen rose lovers who, after entering a show for the first time, cannot now be kept away, stating they have learned more by entering into competition than they ever thought possible.

So let us have a look at shows and what it means for the competitor. It is better to be forewarned than to be disqualified because you did not know.

 First a piece of root was laid across this modern pottery container with two openings. The right opening finally being filled with white *Iceberg* roses in a slanting style

The show schedule

Study the show schedule very carefully and decide which class or classes you would like to enter. It is better not to enter in more than you can comfortably execute. Read also the regulations, for sometimes it might state that 'No dried foliage' or 'No dyed or surface coloured planet material' is allowed.

You may wish to place some preserved leaves in your arrangement, so you should read the regulations to see if this is allowed. It has now become accepted that 'if it doesn't state you can't, then you can'. Meaning that if the schedule does not prohibit certain items then you can use what you want, remembering the overall principle that plant material should predominate.

As I write, I am looking at the latest schedule of the Royal National Rose Society's show. This will give you an idea of what you might expect if you enter a show at this level. Remember that the word 'Arrangement' has been superceded by the word 'Exhibit' and this word allows you to make an arrangement or composition *with* or *without* accessories. So here follows the title of the show, it begins:

LIVING WITH ROSES

Floral Art Section

Any flowers and foliage may be used unless otherwise stated, but roses must predominate.
Where background is provided the height thereof will be 3 ft 6 in.
THE QUEEN ALEXANDRA MEMORIAL TROPHY

Class A *Living with Roses* A table decoration. No cutlery. Table 6 ft x 3 ft will be provided. Own cloths and skirting may be used

Class B *A New Life* An interpretative exhibit using miniature roses with any foliage but no other flowers. Space 1 ft. Pale turquoise background

Class C *School Life* An interpretative exhibit. Space 3 ft. Brown background

Class D *The Good Life*   An interpretative exhibit.
Space 3 ft. Lime green background

Class E *That's Life*   An interpretative exhibit.
Space 3 ft. Cream background

Class F *Church Life*   An exhibit for a church window.
No accessories.
Space 4 ft 6 in. Pale turquoise background

Class G *Married Life*   A humorous interpretative exhibit.
Space 4 ft. Gold background

Class H *Still Life*   An interpretative exhibit.
Space 3 ft. Brown background

Class I *Night Life*   An interpretative exhibit.
Space 3 ft. Dark green background

In classes J-L the roses must be obtained from the exhibitor's
own garden.

Class J *Wild Life*   A free standing exhibit.
Space 3 ft. No background provided or allowed

Class K *Sporting Life*   An interpretative exhibit.
Space 4 ft. Lime green background

Class L *Memories of Life*   An exhibit using Old Garden
Roses and rose foliage only.
Space 3 ft. Cream background

An invitation to branches of the Women's Institute or
Townswomen's Guilds.

Class M *Village Life*   A composite craft exhibit which must
include two flower arrangements, roses to predominate.
Space 4 ft 6 in. Lime green background

Having decided upon the classes you intend to enter, pack all the items, mechanics and accessories you might require. Transport your roses, either upright in a bucket of water, or packed tightly in a box, covered with plastic. The more tightly they are packed the better, it avoids them tumbling about, so bruising the petals.

1 Make sure you are interpreting the title of the class correctly. For instance, if the class title is *Fire over England*, it would not be advisable to use your favourite pink and white roses, for the judges will be looking for orange, flame and red roses to interpret such a title. Your pink and white roses could be reserved for another class, such as *My Favourite Roses* or *A Ballet Scene*.

2 Make sure your *design* will fill two thirds of the niche or space allowed. Try not to have all your roses low down, leaving the top part of the niche empty, nor even have them all to one side leaving the other side empty. This comes under the heading of *proportion*, ie scaling ones roses to each other, and to the vase and the whole to the niche.

3 Good *design* is very important. Whatever shape you might make, the stems should be unified at a certain point which is usually emphasised by either larger roses or leaves, or fruit if it is allowed.

4 *Colour* is also important. This does not mean harmony or your personal choice of colour, but your choice of colour in interpreting the title. For instance, if there were a class entitled *Sleeping Beauty*, you might use grey and pale pink or

This attractive figurine stands in the centre of a James Naylor ring filled with *Oasis* into which pale pink and cream roses were inserted. Short stems of pale green Alchemilla mollis break up the sameness of the roses and the whole stands on a pale green base. This is ideal for a table centrepiece. If the ring is unobtainable stand the figurine in a large plate or small tray surrounded by wet *Oasis* into which the roses can be inserted

white roses, whereas if the title was *The War of the Roses*, you naturally would use red and white roses. So do study the title of the class, then choose your colours.

5 The *quality* or *condition* of your roses will also be taken into account by the judges. They will not be looked upon as being perfect horticultural specimens, but they will be noticed for their quality and condition, so do give them a deep drink the night before as previously stated.

6 Accessories are important. Today, the schedules are much more simple than they were even a few years ago. Nearly always only the title of the class is given which leaves you to interpret it how you wish, or the words 'An *exhibit* to illustrate a certain title' is stated. The word 'exhibit' means 'an arrangement with or without accessories'. If the organisers do not wish to see accessories in certain classes they will state so with the words 'Accessories not allowed'. Accessories, however, do help you to give the meaning to your interpretation, BUT they should be in proportion to the size of the exhibit and also in the spirit of the meaning, ie you would not put your favourite black ebony elephant as an accessory in a *Rose Garden* class, but you would be correct in including it in a class entitled *Sri Lanka*. The accessory should not overpower the rest of your design and, if possible, it should be integrated in the design and not just put at the side as though it was an afterthought. Flowers should always predominate in show work.

 The top of this vase was filled with wet *Oasis* (crumpled wire netting is an alternative) and the asymmetrical outline was made by inserting stems of Philadelphus (syringa). Clusters of white *Iceberg* roses were inserted in the centre

Containers

The type of container should also be taken into consideration. The colour, shade, and texture of your container will all help your exhibit to be observed as a whole. *Sparkling Bright* could be illustrated with a glass or silver container, whereas in a class for *A Trellissed Garden*, a pottery or wooden container would be more appropriate.

Finally, is there some point of distinction that can raise *your* exhibit a few points above the others? Every other point may be perfect, but a good artistic judge, if faced with several of fairly equal merits will look for some point of distinction, some spark of inspiration that will give it an extra lift. It may be the placement of the accessory or the addition of some striped leaves to lighten a dark effect. The title might be painted in a small frame encircled with dry flowers, berries might be added as focal interest, but whatever it is, a good judge will discover it.

All of this might sound daunting but it need not be, for after reading through these hints a few times, it all becomes automatic, which will leave you free, when at the show, to be creative, and with today's schedules you can be as creative as you feel, for there is very little in the conditions to stop you.

So, in assessing the points the judges will look for; they will take into account

1 whether the exhibit interprets the title of the class.
2 Good design, which includes the proportion and scale.
3 Colour.
4 Condition of plant material.
5 Suitability of container.
6 Suitability of accessories.
7 Point of distinction.

Of course, there will never be full agreement among judges or competitors to the correct judgement of artistic arrangements – so much depends upon mood, taste, even emotion, but a good judge is usually objective and is qualified for her Knowledge, Fairness, Experience, Impartiality, Courage and Tact.

 This simple design for the home is composed with the attractive flat-headed *Rosemary Rose,* held in a silver teapot in clear water. It is suitable for any position in the home

Judging

There are some who contend that art should not be judged, yet all art is judged or assessed in some way or another whether it is by the extent of its appreciation or by the amount an artist's work sells. Even at great art exhibitions all over the world some form of judgement takes place by the hanging committee and the final judgement on any creative work on show (and flower arranging *is* creative) is whether other people like it and want it. And it seems at the main Rose shows that people do want it, for crowds now attend these exhibitions and delight in passing their approval. Yet, it was in 1899 that the Royal National Rose Society in England, which has been organising Rose shows since 1858, first introduced classes for rose decorations and they have continued to do so ever since, believing as I do, that there is no greater stimulus to advancement in any field than that of competition.

 An interesting piece of root, picked from upturned tree, is here placed across the rim of the modern pottery container which holds a pinholder. Tall stems of Sisyrinchium stratum were inserted for height and a few pink roses were placed low down. Water, of course, was added

Rose Recipes -
old and new

Rose hip jelly or marmalade

Allow half a pint of water to every pound of rose hips and boil
until tender. Pass the pulp through a sieve thus holding back
the pips. Add one pound of preserving sugar to each pound
of pulp and boil until it jellies when tested on a cold saucer.
It is full of vitamin C.

Those interested in rose hip jelly making should certainly
grow *Rosa Moyesii* for its prolific bottle shaped hips. *Rosa
Rubrifolia*, loved for its long swerving branches of leaves,
also produces masses of berries, whilst *Rosa Frau Dagmar
Hartopp* will give small round apple like hips.

Rose petal jelly
Ingredients:
Dried rose petals
Preserving sugar
Apples

Method: Make apple jelly with good cooking apples but do
not peel them. Cut them up fairly small and put them in a
preserving pan and cover with cold water. Simmer slowly to a
pulp. Strain the pulp through a jelly bag and leave to drip all
night. Measure the liquid and to every pint allow a pound of
preserving sugar. Stir until the sugar is dissolved then put in
as many dried rose petals as the liquid will hold. Boil till the
jelly sets when tested on a cold saucer. Strain before potting.

 The full-petalled hybrid tea rose *Stanley Gibbons* is here used on a pinholder in a shallow dish of water placed at the side of a basket tray. Variegated privet (Ligustrum) back the roses and give added interest

73

Candied rose petals

Dip small rose petals in beaten egg white or weak gum arabic and lay on a greaseproof paper sheet covered with castor sugar. Then sprinkle the petals both sides with sugar, leaving them to dry in a warm place or cool oven. These can be stored in a jar with sheets of paper in between layers to be used for decoration on cakes or as sweet meats. A few spots of cochineal added to the egg whites will help the rose colouring.

Rose petal and honey sandwiches

Pick scented rose petals and after removing the white heel, finely chop the petals and mix with thick honey for a sandwich spread which children love. The petals have a vitamin C content.

Sauce eglantine

This sauce, which is excellent to serve with roast lamb, etc., was frequently made at Balmoral in Queen Victoria's time.
Ingredients:
Sweet briar hips; Lemon juice
Method: Remove all the seeds from the hips and then make a purée of them with as little water as possible. Sweeten to taste and add a squeeze of lemon juice. I have made this and added a little gelatine.

Julia's Rose, the new parchment-brown rose, which won the Gold Medal at the 1983 World Congress of Roses, is here used in a modern pottery container by Ivy Denner. A large pinholder was placed in the bottom of the container across which a dry twisted branch was placed. The roses were then cut to different lengths and inserted each below the other with short ones at the back

Rose trifle

Cut sponge fingers or slices in half, coat with rose petal jam and arrange in a large glass dish. Pour over them sufficient rose wine or any vin rosé to hand to soak them. Add a little raspberry juice to the wine for extra effect if desired. Then cover with a pink blancmange, or custard made with eggs, and colour with a few drops of cochineal. Sprinkle with chopped almonds and add some ratafia biscuits, finally cover with whipped cream and decorate with crystallized rose petals. (*Author's recipe 1956*)

Rose water

Cover two pounds of scented red petals with cold water and bring slowly to the boil. At near boiling point, take off heat and leave to cool, then strain the water. This gives a pink perfumed water to add to guests' wash basins.

Rose vinegar

A jar filled with rose petals should be covered with white wine vinegar and left for 48 hours, preferably in the sun. When the liquid is strained off it is most cooling and refreshing when used on the forehead and hands.

Morning rose cocktail

21g – ¾ oz of white rum
21g – ¾ oz of Curacao
14g – ½ oz of Grenadine
14g – ½ oz fresh lemon juice
Shake well with cracked ice and serve

 Dry twisted honeysuckle branch was laid across the top of these cluster pots, the top one of which held a pinholder and water. Sprays of rose foliage inserted for a curved outline, and *Doris Tysterman* roses were inserted for main interest. Low roses should flow forward

Rose petal wine

Pick rose petals of the most perfumed varieties (see page 90), when they are in full bloom, and place a quart – 1 litre measureful into a quart – 1 litre of boiling water. After steeping for five minutes, squeeze these through a cloth or jelly bag. Discard the used petals, bring liquid to boil again and infuse a further similar quantity. Repeat this three or four times until the liquid has a strong enough scent. Now add 1 lb – 454g of white sugar and boil gently for ten minutes, skimming off any scum which rises. Pour into a crock, basin or stone jar and add a little less than a quarter of an ounce – 5g of baker's yeast, previously thinned with a few drops of water.

Cover and tie down with two or three layers of cotton material, eg a teacloth, as this will keep the insects away but allow carbon dioxide gas to escape. Leave in a warm place, such as the kitchen, until the working of the yeast has ceased. This can be some weeks, but you will know when it happens as the liquid will no longer hiss and bubble.

I find a gallon – 4.5 litres is the best quantity to make at a time and if you have not an old crock or flagon, sometimes a glass winchester from the hairdresser or grocer is obtainable, and a special fermentation air lock can be obtained from *Messrs Ferris*, Portland Square, Bristol 2. They also supply all kinds of equipment for home wine making. Another useful address for home wine makers is the *Grey Owl Research Laboratories*, Almondsbury, nr Bristol, who supply a wine yeast and a sherry yeast, the latter being better for rose hips which make a good sherry production.

This white design is created by first filling the vase with a block of water-soaked *Oasis* (soak for half an hour), or crumpled wire netting could be used, then making the outline off centre with stems of fine Stephanandra foliage and spray carnations. Lilies and white *Iceberg* roses, which are so prolific in summer, were placed in the centre making sure the lower ones protruded forward over the rim

Summer rose petal cup

Place two large handfuls of fresh rose petals in a basin, cover with a large cupful of icing sugar and leave for 30 minutes. Then pour over a large bottle of Vichy water and a tablespoonful of lemon juice and place the bowl in the refrigerator. Before serving, slightly press and strain into a punch bowl or large jug, adding a bottle of sparkling wine, three bottles of sweet white wine and one bottle of dry wine. This will fill about 72 glasses. Serve with fresh rose petals floating on the surface.

How to preserve whole roses

'Dip a rose that is neither in the bud nor overblown in a sirup, consisting of sugar, double refined and rose-water boiled to his full height, then open the leaves one by one with a fine smooth bodkin either of bone or wood; and presently if it be a hot sunny day, and whilst the sunne is in goode height, lay them on papers in the sunne or else dry them with some gentle heat in a close roome, heating the roome before you set them in, or in an oven upon papers in pewter dishes and then put them up in glasses; and keepe them in dry cupboards neere the fire; you must take out the seeds, if you meane to eat them. You may proove this preserving with sugar-candy instead of sugar, if you please.' Sir Hugh Platt, *Delights for Ladies*, 1594.

Preserved roses for flowering in winter

Before the days of the hybrid tea roses, in fact as early as medieval times, it was customary to preserve roses in order to have them in flower at Christmas time. Today, many of us in Britain can pick garden roses during December but should

 Four dried Strelitzia leaves were gilded and inserted on a pinholder placed in the top of the pottery container. One *Peace* rose was inserted for final effect. When using dry items in water, bind them first with clear adhesive tape to avoid their softening in water

you wish to preserve some summer roses you should cut long stemmed buds which are just opening and showing colour. After giving them a long drink, dip each stem end in melted candle wax to seal it and wrap each one separately in tissue paper before closing them in an airtight tin, box or plastic food container. Keep in a cool dry place or fridge, about 50°F – 10°C and when required cut off the waxed portion of the stems placing them in warm water where the buds will slowly open. I would think that a polythene bag would do equally well as a tin, but I have not yet tried this.

A modern method of drying roses

*From the chemist or use powdered borax

Sprinkle a half inch – 12mm layer of powdered silica gel* in a box, such as a shoe box, and lay the rose upon it. Several can be laid side by side or three heads on one end and three more the other. Then cover the roses completely with more powder, aiming to get some in between the petals and leave for a week, after which the moisture would have been absorbed and the roses will be dry, although some loss of bright colour will be noticeable. If you want to store these dried roses until winter keep them in a box in which a little of the powder is placed to absorb any moisture that is in the atmosphere. If you wish to preserve more opened roses place the stems through holes in a piece of cardboard, the blooms remaining above the cardboard with the stems reaching down into a box. Then with a spoon cover the rose heads with the powder making sure you surround the lower petals to give support, then place the powder in between and around all the petals until they are completely covered. Semi-full blooms should be used and not fully blown ones, for if the bees have done their work on the roses, the petals will drop in any case.

Twisted and flocked bamboo give height to this modern design using *Queen Elizabeth* roses. The roses are cut to different levels and held on a large pinholder in a shallow glass dish which stands on a perspex disc, and which in turn stands on an upturned glass goblet

To make rose beads for a rosary

'Gather the roses on a dry sunny day and chop the petals
finely. Put them in a saucepan and barely cover with water.
Heat for about an hour but do not let the mixture boil.
Repeat this process for the three days and if necessary add
more water. The deep black beads made from rose petals are
made this rich colour by warming in a rusty pan. It is
important never to let the mixture boil but each day to warm
it to a moderate heat. Make the beads by working the pulp
with the fingers into balls. When thoroughly well worked
and fairly dry press on to a bodkin to make the holes in the
centres of the beads. Until they are perfectly dry the beads
have to be moved frequently on the bodkin or they will be
difficult to remove without breaking them. Held for a few
moments in a warm hand these beads give out a pleasing
fragrance.' *Nineteenth century recipe*

Bags to scent linen

'Take rose petals dried in the shade, cloves beaten to a gross
powder and mace scraped; mix them together and put the
composition into little bags.' (*Temple of Flora*)

A bag to smell unto,
or to cause one to sleep

'Take dried Rose leaves, keep them close in a glasse which
will keep them sweet, then take powder of Mints, powder of
Cloves in a grosse powder. Put the same to the Rose leaves,
then put all these together in a bag, and take that to bed with
you and it will cause you to sleepe, and it is good to smell
unto at other times.' (*Ram's Little Dodoen*, 1606)

 Picked in late September the scented *Lady Seton* rose is
here held in the cup of this gilded container. Most hybrid
tea roses, as well as others, bloom twice in the season

Rose scented candles

Melt left-over candle ends (white) in a double boiler. Skim off the wick pieces and for every pound of wax obtained stir in half a cupful of very finely crushed dried rose petals. Different coloured roses, especially the reds and pinks, will give an attractive mottled effect. Fasten some wick or coarse loose twine to a nail to hold it in place at the bottom of a tin, or other waxed mould, and hold the wick firmly as you pour the wax, to keep it centred.

Rose scented tea

Add fresh or dried rose petals to the tea in your tea caddy to give your tea a subtly different flavour.

A few modern tips

Rose petals left to soak in rainwater makes a soft perfumed yet stimulating hair rinse.

Try adding a touch of rose perfume or bath oil to electric light bulbs *before* switching on the lights for a party.

A handful of rose bath salts in a small bowl of hot water will scent a whole room. As also will a few drops of rose bath oil shaken into a small bowl of boiling water.

Add a few drops of rose water to your lingerie rinse water for a subtle delicate fragrance.

Sprinkle rose water on the ironing board before pressing lingerie or blouses.

This simple design in a moon-shaped container is composed of fine willow tendrils for height and five *Beautiful Britain* roses, the lower one pointing forward over the rim

Pot pourri

Yet, though thou fade,
From thy dead leaves let fragrance rise;
Go, lovely rose

HENRY K. WHITE 1785-1806

Many have their own favourite recipe for pot pourri. Here is mine, though I am inclined to change it now and again, adding more grated orange one year and less spicc, or more clove and less lavender.

Gather highly scented roses, the Centifolias and Damask roses are excellent. Spread out the petals to dry, either on muslin or thin paper, and place in a box or jar until all the ingredients have been gathered and dried. Rose petals should form the bulk, then add dry lavender flowers and any other strong smelling flowers such as heliotrope, honeysuckle, clove pinks, and jasmine. I always add the leaves of mint, verbena scented geranium, rosemary and bay, and slightly crush these when dry. Add the grated rind of an orange and lemon and a dessertspoonful of orris root as a fixative, then, when all the ingredients are dry, mix in a basin and leave to rest, stirring occasionally.

Place in open bowls or jars around the home and after some time, when the scent fades, a few spots of oil of roses or lavender can be added, or there is an excellent *Taylor's* pot pourri reviver on the market today.

This Meissen compote-style container was filled with a block of water-soaked *Oasis* pressed on to a pinholder for stability. Tall delphiniums and spray carnations form the height and width of the arrangement whilst *Champagne* roses are placed centrally. Small *Garnette* roses and pinks plus blue cornflowers were inserted for filling, each stem aimed towards the centre, the lower stems tilting slightly forward and over the rim. Similar flowers were added at the back to give a three-dimensional effect

The Perfume of the Rose

Most recipes, pot pourris and other uses of the rose require a high percentage of perfume, so I asked some of my friends in the Rose World, which rose, in their opinion, they consider the most highly scented bloom. Of course it is difficult to reduce a choice to one rose, but here is a list from those who should know.

Mr E F Allen, MA Dip Agric (Cantab), Hon Scientific Adviser to the Royal National Rose Society, chooses *Papa Meilland* as a Hybrid Tea and *Michelle* as a floribunda

Mr H Anderson, a famous Scottish rosegrower, chooses *My Love*

Mr R C Balfour, MBE, DHM, President of the World Federation of Rose Societies, Past President of the Royal National Rose Society, chooses *Crimson Glory* which he says blooms from late May until Christmas

Mr Frank Fryer, of Fryers Nurseries Limited, Knutsford, chooses *Double Delight*

Mr Harold Goldstein, Executive Director of the American Rose Society also lists *Double Delight,* not only for its fragrance but for its beauty

Roses, in view of their strong appeal, make ideal additions to arrangements of mixed summer flowers. Here they are used in the low centre of this slightly off-centre design of white stock, paeonies, pinks and gypsophila, all held in wet *Oasis* in a white china container. Trails of greenery soften the outline and, by drooping down, unite the flowers to the vase

Mr A C Gregory (Tony) Grower and Breeder of the Rose Gardens, Stapleford, Nottingham, chooses *Crimson Glory*

Mr Jack Harkness, Breeder and Author, of R Harkness and Co Ltd, Hitchin, Herts, chooses *Margaret Merrill* for its refreshing scent in preference to a heavy scent. Runner up, *Fragrant Cloud*

Mr W R Le Grice, of Le Grice Rose Growers and Nurseryman of Norfolk, chooses *Fragrant Cloud.* The firm specialises in roses of unusual colours

John Mattock of the Rose Nurseries, Nuneham Courtenay, nr Oxford, Rose Grower, Breeder and Council member of the Royal Horticultural Society, chooses a Bourbon rose, *Madame Isaac Periere*

Madame Louisette Meilland, of *Peace* rose fame and, with Mr Alain Meilland, heads of the French rose breeder firm at Cap d'Intibbes, lists *Papa Meilland* as her favourite

Mr Sean McCann of Dublin, rose writer for *Garden News,* columnist for *The American Rose,* and author of *All the World's Roses,* chooses *Mr Lincoln*

Mr Sam McGredy, breeder, formerly of Northern Ireland, now of New Zealand, chooses *Fragrant Cloud*

The Marchioness of Salisbury, famous for her gardens at historical Hatfield House, Hertfordshire, chooses an old shrub rose *Kazanlik*

Mr R D Squires, President of the National Rose Society (1983) and amateur rose grower, lists *Margaret Merrill,* with *Conrad F Meyer* as runner up

Mr A S Thomas, OBE, VME, DHM, Author and Vice President of Royal National Rose Society of Melbourne, Australia, lists *Ellen Mary* as his choice

Graham S Thomas, OBE, VHM, VMM, Garden Consultant to the National Trust and author of several gardening classics on Shrub roses Perrennials, etc, chooses *Maiden's Blush* from among many he would like to include

 This modern design in a Clive Brooker pottery container was given height by stems of fasciated willow inserted on to a pinholder in the top of the container. A piece of root wood hung downwards fixed by wire and the parchment *Julia's Rose* was inserted as main interest

I recommend *Find that Rose,* which is a most useful pamphlet by the rose Growers Association. It lists in alphabetical order all the varieties that are grown by the members of the Association. It is obtainable from Mr P Harkness, The Rose Gardens, Hitchin, Hertfordshire, England.

Water-soaked *Oasis* pressed on to a pinholder for stability was placed in a shallow dish of water standing on a white china cake stand to form the basis for this dainty arrangement composed of mauve Hosta Lily flowers for height, with pinks and other small flowers for width. The pink *Garnette* roses were inserted in the centre making sure the low ones flowed forward. Water should always be added daily to *Oasis* when used in an arrangements

The Naming of a Rose

Many people ask what or who decides how a rose is to be named. Is it by chance, design or purpose? They ask, 'Did Margot Fonteyn agree to the lovely red rose named after her?' and did the grower have a certain ballerina in mind when the dainty pink rose. *Ballerina,* was bred? Who decided that a rose should be named *Whisky Mac* and why? And who was Joey in that lovely peach/flame-coloured rose *Just Joey.* Was it a dog or a parrot or perhaps a child? And who is Stella?

Many of us know or can guess that commercial organisations will pay vast sums for the privilege of having a rose named after one of their products. Sometimes they purchase thousands of bushes for distribution to their customers, at other times they are satisfied by the huge advertisement they receive through the catalogues and growers.

Names of roses are given to certain personalities in return for the publicity that the name will attract, for if the name of the personality is recognisable by tens of thousands of people, this will help the sales. Many breeders of roses name their roses after members of their families, others perhaps for a sentimental reason, but no matter what the reason every name has to be registered in the Royal National Rose Society in conjunction with the International Rose Society.

 Using a collander filled with *Oasis* tied up with ribbon, short stems of the floribunda *Super Star* roses were inserted all round. A similar bow attached to a wire or strong hairpin was inserted at the base. A square block of *Oasis* covered with wire netting could act as an alternative holder

Here a tiny silver salt cellar is used to hold these *Boule de Neige* miniature roses. Charming for a guest room or a wine table

Facts and Fancies about Roses
historical, legendary, traditional and literary

The rose is a universal phenomenon appearing in the legends, fiction, history and botany of most countries of the world. The more you read, whether your tastes lead you to religion, travel, fairy tales or accomplishments, the more you are sure to discover about the rose.

My own research has been very rewarding and of great fascination, in fact after a few days of reading I have found myself, when in a group of friends, saying, 'do you know…' and then I have quoted some recently acquired fact about the rose. The phrase 'Do you know' is a very useful opening to conversation, so in the event of roses being your particular interest, I here set out in short phrases a number of facts and fancies which might interest and please you.

Homer, the celebrated Greek poet about 900 BC, alluded to the rose in the *Illiad* and *Odyssey*. This is the earliest written record of the flower.

The highest praise Homer could offer to beauty was to resemble it to a rose.

The Rose is associated with Love. Always with Venus, the Goddess of Love, for legend states that the rose was the gift of God to celebrate Venus rising from the sea. Immortalised by Botticelli's painting *The Birth of Venus* in Uffizi Gallery, Florence.

Roses became the sacred flowers of Venus and again, according to legend, Cupid as a bribe consecrated them to Hippocrates, the God of Silence, in order to keep him quiet and prevent him from revealing the indiscretions of Venus. From then on the rose became an emblem of Silence.

In 477 BC a *secret* meeting was held in the Temple of Minerva under a bower of roses. Thus the word 'sub rosa' means in secret and there is an ancient custom of having a rose suspended over the council table to indicate that all present are sworn to secrecy.

The Jacobite rose

 Roses are beautiful in themselves without thought of design. Prepare the roses well and choose a colour scheme to complement the vase or container. Cut the stems to different lengths to allow each head to be seen. Here the Dresden vase was filled with crumpled wire netting held down with an elastic band and, after removing the thorns and splitting the stem ends, the roses inserted in a semi-diagonal line

The rose was adopted by the followers of Bonnie Prince Charlie (1744-1761) to typify the fact that only 'sub rosa' could the Jacobites (followers of James – Latin: Jacobus – the father of Prince Charles) labour faithfully in the cause.

Not everyone is aware, even today, that in Midsummer, the two new Sheriffs of the City of London are about to be elected by the Liverymen, the Lord Mayor and all former Sheriffs and others present in the Assembly, are asked to retire, preceded by the City Marshal and the Sword Bearer to the Livery Hall whilst awaiting the result of the election. To show that the proceedings are in secret, it is here that the sword is placed on a bed of red and white rose petals; red and white being the City of London colours.

For the same reason, the roofs of many confessional boxes in Roman Catholic Churches are decorated with roses.

Up to quite recent times, a rose decoration in the dining room ceiling was a gracious invitation to talk freely without fear of it being repeated, but this custom, alas, is no longer observed.

The delicate use of a rose tucked behind or over a lady's ear signifies that words whispered are for her ears only.

A few short stems from the very short *Lady Taylor* floribunda rose are placed centrally, backed by twisty stems of summer Jasmine polyanthum. The top of this Wedgwood glass candlestick was filled with water-soaked floral foam, and the Jasmine was first inserted followed by the roses. This new short rose is superb in the garden, growing no taller than 18 inches (46 cm).

A week after this picture was taken the Jasmine opened its star-like petals

 Suitable for any small table, this china basket holds stems of *Pink Grootendorst* which has fimbriated petals, and a few cream old fashion shrub roses. These old fashioned roses, so popular at the moment, need only to be casually placed. Remove the thorns, split the stem ends and fill the container with crumpled wire netting and water before arranging

 A large bowl of mixed cream and pink roses including *Peace* is placed behind the sofa in this elegant drawing room. The stems were held by crumpled wire netting

The rose is mentioned in the Bible in connection with Isiah:
'The Wilderness shall blossom as a Rose'.

In the Apocryphal scriptures the son of Sirach likens Wisdom to a rose plant in Jericho and Holiness to a rose growing by a brook of the field.

The rose still blooms in the Garden of Gethsemane, Palestine.

*The Rose of Sharon, Aaron's Beard, is really Hypericum calycinum – *RHS Dictionary of Gardening*. Most of us know the foot-high evergreen with yellow flowers, blooming from June to September, which flourishes even under trees.

In the biblical references to the Rose of Jericho and the Rose of Sharon, many have tried to prove the name 'rose' to be incorrect in these instances. However, it is mentioned in the *Book of Wisdom* ii, 8. 'Let us crown ourselves with rosebuds before they are withered.' In the *Song of Songs* the Church compares herself unto the 'Rose of Sharon'. Sharon is a plain to the west of Jerusalem, noted for its beauty and fertility.*

Climbing or rambler roses are ideal when a flowing swerve is required especially when using a tall pedestal. Here in a white painted iron lamp stand a bowl was placed containing a block of wet *Oasis* pressed on to a pinholder. The tallest sprays were placed upwards and flowing downwards with the shorter stems being used for filling in. Always allow some roses to flow forward and backwards to avoid a flat effect

Confuscius (551 BC) discussing in the Analects questions of beauty:
Dimples playing in a witching smile
Beautiful eyes so dark, so bright!
Oh and her face may be thought the while
Coloured by art, red rose on white!

Syria, according to some writers, took its name from *Suri,* a species of rose indigenous to that country.

In the Rose Feasts of Nero, that luxurious tyrant, is pictured necklaced and crowned with flowers, lying on pillows stuffed with roses and petals strewing the floor, whilst fountains flung up rose water. Suetonius, a Latin writer credits Nero with spending something like the equivalent of £30,000 on roses for one feast. Wine was flavoured with roses, a rose pudding was served, and before and after the feast guests bathed in marble lined pools filled with water perfumed with roses.

At the beginning of the nineteenth century, the Empress Josephine of France sent messengers to every corner of Europe in order to secure all known varieties of the Rose. She planted the famous rose gardens at the Palace of Malmaison and this gave the opportunity for study and the final fillip which raised the flower to the extreme popularity it enjoys today.

 This Victorian hand vase holds a bunch of ten *Garnette* roses bought from the florist. Stems cut to different lengths can be held by *Oasis* or wire netting

Although the Greeks were ardent admirers of the rose, the Romans made great advances in its culture and created an industry by their demand for blooms and trees.

The Rose Service, held annually in June, at the Abbey Church of St Alban owes its origins to the phrase 'Amongst the roses of the martyrs, brightly shines St Alban.' Young (and not so young) bring bunches of roses to the service – which is largely for children – and then leave them at the Shrine. The scent of the roses pervades the whole Abbey and it is one of the highlights of a busy season.

There is an eastern tradition which tells us that on Mount Calasay, the Hindu Olympus, there stands a table upon which lies a silver rose, bearing among its petals the two holy servant of the Most High whose duty it is to 'Praise God without ceasing'.

A Mohammedon tradition claims that Mohammed took his famous all night flight through Heaven from Mecca born aloft the back of the supernatural steed Al Borak. Alighting next morning on the Kubbet es Sakra in Jerusalem, from the sacred sweat of the prophet's forehead falling to earth, roses sprang, whilst from the magic sweat of Al Borak came yellow roses.

 A few pink roses from the garden were held in a delicate Meissen shoe for a guest room

The majority of roses in ancient times were cultivated varieties. Horace (65 BC) and Pliny (AD 61) both mention the cultivation of roses.

The rose is reputed to have be born in the East and diffused all over the world. It is found on glaciers, deserts, mountains, in marshes and forests, valleys and plains. In fact, the rose is known to be native to all countries with the exception of South America.

A 'bed of roses' was no idle reference to the Persians who used to employ sacksful of roses to make a perfumed couch.

The rose is a symbol of beauty, often in a superlative sense; such as perfection. Hence 'la vie en Rose' and 'Rose-coloured spectacles' and 'a bed of roses'.

In the early Christian era, Arab and Persian amulets were worn or used to protect their bodies from evil spirits. The ink used by the scribe was sometimes perfumed with oil of roses.

This gilded wall sconce holds a small dish of wet *Oasis* which in turn holds *Contesse Vandal,* pale pink hybrid tea roses. Note the lower which protrude forwards. Ideal for a party effect when guests are standing

114

St Rose – Rose, Saint of Lima (1586-1617) was the first canonised saint of the New World. Born in Lima, Peru, where she lived till her death, she became a Dominican tertiary in her twentieth year and lived a life of great austerity and religious devotion. She was canonised by Clement X in 1671. Her feast is observed on 30 August.

Step 1   Place a glass dish holding a pinholder or floral foam in the top of a glass fish bowl. Insert tall stem of orange coloured Euphorbia fulgents for height and low swerve, followed by Eucalyptus leaves

Step 2   Add yellow roses, each cut to a different length, and unite all the stems with cyclamen foliage, or any other at hand. Add water to the dish

The fish bowl can be filled with coloured water: pink, red or yellow according to the roses used.

The name *Dog Rose (Rosa sempervirens)* is understood to
have come about from the belief that its roots were a cure for
hydrophobia, ie rabies.

Although rose hips have been used for many ailments
throughout history, it was not until the middle 1900s that
their high vitamin C content was recognised which proved so
valuable in Britain during the Second World War when
hundreds of tons of rose hips were collected to make rose
hip syrup.

In Astrology, the planet Venus governs all sweet smelling
flowers and herb especially the Rose.

Each year in early September in West Grove, Pennsylvania,
one red rose is presented to a direct descendant of William
Penn, the founder of the State of Pennsylvania, by the growers
of Star Roses, as a quit rent for their having purchased a plot
of land on which stood an old inn an history land mark begun
in 1740.

In 1731 the deeds of the property were handed down to
the grandson of William Penn, and after searching the
archives it was discovered that whoever became the owners
of the property should pay the annual rent of one red rose
instead of, in ancient times, laying down the sword of the
Feudal overlord. The Conrad Pyle Company, growers of Star
Roses, keep up this delightful tradition with a Red Rose Rent
Day celebrations which includes speakers and Rose
Arrangements.

 Crumpled wire netting (2 in. – 50 cm mesh) is pressed
into the top of this pewter tankard standing on a pewter
plate. The white moss roses, *Blanche Moreau*, are
inserted through the wire into the water and make a
pretty sight for all rose lovers

A similar, but older ceremony is staged each year in the City of London on Midsummer's day when a rose, presented to the Lord Mayor on a cushion, is paid as a quit rent by a descendant or one appointed of Sir Robert Knollys, as a fine for his wife having built a *haut pas* over a road without permission. The full story of the reason for this act is disclosed in my *Flower Arrangers Bedside Book*.

In Peru it is understood that Eve of the Garden of Eden sinned not for plucking an apple, but a rose.

By successfully answering questions on the Rose in 1956, Mr Albert Norman of Surrey, England, won Independent Television's biggest money prize in the *64,000 Dollar Question* quiz programme.

Poets and writers found constant inspiration in the rose, and playwrights from Shakespeare to the present day never fail to find a theme in connection with the rose. Shakespeare mentioned the rose more than a hundred times in his plays and lines similar to these are typical of his writings:

The rose looks fair, but fairer we it deem
For that sweet odour which doth in it live.

Sonnet LIV

... that which we call a rose,
By any other name would smell as sweet.

Romeo and Juliet

 Any hybrid tea roses of any colour can be used in this manner for a floor standing arrangement. A jar of water was placed inside the pottery plant container and the roses need only to be casually placed as long as no two heads fall evenly with the other. Prepare the roses as on page 20

Roses have been featured by so many song writers that I tried to check some records. I found it was estimated that there are more than four thousand songs, among which are favourites such as *Roses of Picardy, The Rose of Tralee, My Irish Rose, Only a Rose* and the *Last Rose of Summer*.

The famous Rose Window in York Minster measures 22 ft 4 in. in diameter. Other large Rose windows are to be seen in both Chartres and Notre Dame Cathedrals in France and the beautiful modern Rose window is housed in Lancing College, Sussex.

The theatre has also attracted reference to the Rose with Clifford Bax's play *A Rose Without a Thorn* and the ballet *Spectre de la Rose* which was an adaption of Gautier's poem drew tens of thousands during its many performances. Anderson and Grimm featured the rose in many of the Fairy Tales and Oscar Wilde's famous fairy story 'The Nightingale and the Rose' appeals to many for its sadness.

Floribunda roses are here placed in a low triangular design in a white metal container. If the heads of floribunda roses are too heavy it is wise to remove some of the more open flowers which will give room for others to open

I am sure many readers of this book will have Rose stories of their own, but one more remains vividly in my mind ever since I was given a glass goblet in Czechoslovakia engraved with a rose and the name of *Lidice*. Lidice, as many will know was the name of a mining village, north west of Prague which was completely oblitered, even from the records by the Germans on 10 June 1942 when they shot all the males (200) and deported all the women, many to Ravensbruck concentration camp in reprisal for the assasination of Reinhard Heydrich, the German representative in the Protectorate. The children of the village were sent to German institutions, many disappearing without trace. In 1947 a new village was designated nearby and a museum, a monument, and an international rose garden marks the sight of the original village. Many British miners attended the ceremony of the laying of the foundation stone. Hence the *Lidice Rose*.

Appendix

SPECIALIST ROSE GROWERS

Great Britain

Anderson's Rose Nurseries
  Friarsfield Road, Cults, Aberdeen
Apuldram Manor Farm
  Chichester, Sussex
Armstrong's Roses
  West-Winds, 15 Knockboy Road, Broughshane, Co. Antrim,
  Northern Ireland
J Bradshaw & Son
  Busheyfields Nursery, Herne, Herne Bay, Kent
Burston Nurseries Ltd
  North Orbital Road, St Albans, Herts
Cants of Colchester Ltd
  The Old Rose Gardens, Stanway, Colchester, Essex CO3 5UP
Caldwell & Sons Ltd
  The Nurseries, Chelford Road, Knutsford, Cheshire
  WA16 8LX
James Cocker & Sons
  Rose Specialist, Whitemyres, Lang Stracht, Aberdeen
D & W Croll Ltd
  Dalhousie Nurseries, Broughty Ferry, Dundee
Mark Court Thanet Roses
  Pyson's Road, Broadstairs, Kent CT10 2LA
Fryer's Nurseries Ltd
  Manchester Road, Knutsford, Cheshire
Gandy's Roses Ltd
  North Kilworth, Lutterworth, Leics

Goodinsons Roses Ltd
   Bingley Lane Nurseries, Stannington, Sheffield, Yorks
Gregory's Roses
   The Rose Gardens, Stapleford, Nottingham
R Harkness & Co Ltd
   The Rose Gardens, Hitchin, Herts
Highfield Nurseries
   Whitminster, Gloucester
Arthur Higgs Roses
   Water Lane Farm, North Hykeham, Lincs
Hill Park Nurseries
   Kingston By Pass, Surbiton, Surrey
Hortico
   Spalding, Lincs
Hyrons Nursery & Garden Centre
   Woodside Road, Amersham, Bucks
C & K Jones
   1 North Street, Sandycroft, Deeside, Clwyd
Knights Nurseries
   Hailsham, Sussex
Legrice Roses
   North Walsham, Norfolk
Limes Rose Nursery
   Kelly, Lifton, Devon
John Mattock Ltd
   The Rose Nurseries, Nuneham Courtenay, Oxford
James McIntyre Roses
   Rose Cottage, Main Street, North Leverton, Retford, Notts
Notcutts Nurseries Ltd
   Woodbridge, Suffolk
Oakdale Nurseries (Findern)
   Burton Road, Findern, Derbys
   Enquiries to Mr M J Woodhouse
J B Philp & Son Ltd
   Elm Park Garden Centre, Aldermaston Road, Pamber End,
   Basingstoke, Hants
Rearsby Roses
   14 Church Leys Avenue, Rearsby, Leicester

Rosemary Roses
　　PO Box No 15, The Nurseries, Stapleford Lane, Beeston, Nottingham
St Bridget Nurseries Ltd
　　Old Rydon Lane, Exeter, Devon
Shaw Rose Trees
　　29 Vicarage Road, Willoughton, Gainsborough, Lincs
Spalding Bulb Company
　　Spalding, Lincs
Timmermans Roses
　　Woodborough, Nottingham
John Train & Sons
　　Benston, Tarbolton, Ayrshire, Scotland
Warley Rose Gardens Ltd
　　Warley Street, Gt Warley, Brentwood, Essex
Wheatcroft Roses Ltd
　　Edwalton, Nottingham
Wisbech Plant Company
　　Walton Road, Wisbech, Cambs
Watkins Rose & Garden Centre
　　Kenilworth Road, Hampton-in-Arden, Solihull, West Midlands

United States of America
American Beauty Roses
　　PO Box 1758, Peoria, Illinois 61656
Armstrong Nurseries Inc
　　Box 473, Ontario, California 91761
Conard Pyle Co
　　West Grove, Pennsylvania 19390
Roses by Fred Edmunds
　　6235 South East Kahle Road, Wilsonville, Oregon 97070
Heritage Rose Gardens
　　40350 Wilderness Road, Branscomb, California 95417
Historical Roses Inc
　　1657 West Jackson Street, Painesville, Ohio 44077
Inter-State Nurseries Inc
　　Hamburg, Iowa 51640

Jackson & Perkins Co
   1 Rose Lane, Medford, Oregon 97501
Justice Miniature Roses
   5947 South West Kahle Road, Wilsonville, Oregon 97070
Joseph J. Kern Nursery
   Box 33, Mentor, Ohio 44060
Krider Nursery Inc
   Box 29, Middlebury, Indiana 46540
Mini-Roses
   PO Box 4255, Station A, Dallas, Texas 75208
Moore Miniature Roses
   Sequoia Nursery, 2519 East Noble Avenue, Visalia,
   California 93277
Nor-East Miniature Roses
   58 Hammond Street, Rowley, Massachusetts 01969
Pixie Treasures
   4121 Prospect Avenue, Yorba Linda, California 92686
Roses of Yesterday and Today
   802 Brown's Valley Road, Watsonville, California
   95076-0398
Swim & Weeks
   4759 Philadelphia Street, Ohio, California 91710
Tiny Petals Nursery
   489 Minot Avenue, Chula Vista, California 92010
Wayside Gardens
   Hodges, South Carolina 29695

Canada

Aubin Nurseries Ltd
   PO Box 1089, Carman, Manitoba ROG OJO
Roses by Walter Lemire
   R.R. 1, Oldcastle, Ontario
Mini Rose Nursery
   PO Box 873, Guelph, Ontario N1H 6M6
Pickering Nursery
   670 Kingston Road (Highway 2), Pickering, Ontario
   L1V 1A6
Springwood Miniature Roses
   Box 255, Port Credit, PO, Missassauga, Ontario L5G 4L8

Index